Time to Ignite Your Light!

The little book of sayings, affirmations, and quotes to motivate you today!

Farrah Brown

Renew the View LLC.

First Edition 2023
by Farrah Brown
Renew the View LLC.
https://Renewtheview.co

Time to Ignite Your Light!

Daily Sayings

https://Renewtheview.co

Hello Friends,

I am Farrah Brown, the Founder of **Renew the View, LLC.** As a *mindset coach*, I am passionate about helping clients reach their goals by making a shift in their thought patterns.

In this book, I would like to offer some words of encouragement to ignite the light within you today! Words matter and more importantly, YOU matter.

Enjoy!
Farrah-

Reflection Moment of the day:

Each day, I invite you to take a pause to consider you and the world around you. What comes to mind as you navigate each page? How are you doing today? Are there moments of gratitude? Is Self-compassion needed today? Enjoy this dive into you.

First, believe that you can and then,
YOU WILL!

Reflection Moment of the day:

WHEN FACED WITH ADVERSITY, JUST SIT BACK, AND REMEMBER
WHO YOU ARE –

AMAZING!

Reflection Moment of the day:

The secret to unlocking your potential is to take the first step!

-

Then the real work begins!

Reflection Moment of the day:

Minding your mind is part of your wellness journey. So, peek in for a change.

Reflection Moment of the day:

Know what was behind you,
Believe what is in front of you,
Trust in the great possibilities ahead of you!

Reflection Moment of the day:

Storms are a good reminder that better things are to come!

Reflection Moment of the day:

The more steps you take,
the more progress you'll make!

Reflection Moment of the day:

> Self-care means that YOU care.
> Dare to care!
> You deserve it!

Reflection Moment of the day:

Your first step can set the tone of the day.
So, make the right move – you got this!

Reflection Moment of the day:

Remember, you have gifts that only YOU can offer!
So, go out there and be all of YOU today!

Reflection Moment of the day:

Hey,
even the smallest efforts count so keep pushing friend!

Reflection Moment of the day:

Change only happens when you put YOUR feet to the ground!

Reflection Moment of the day:

HEY YOU!

This is it!

Today is that day.

Yes! This is,

Your time, Your moment,

<u>YOUR DAY!</u>

Reflection Moment of the day:

Be true to you and walk in the way that God has called you!

Reflection Moment of the day:

Sometimes our motivation can override our ineptness
so now,
there are NO EXCUSES TODAY!

Move Move MOVE!

Reflection Moment of the day:

You have that "fire" that
<u>no one</u>
can extinguish today!

Reflection Moment of the day:

If you put a stake in the ground, you mark the beginning of your success story.

Believe that!

Reflection Moment of the day:

Remember,
YOU set the limit,
not the sky!

Reflection Moment of the day:

There is no better time than now to answer the call to your purpose!

Reflection Moment of the day:

Dreamers and complainers have 1 thing in common – no action.

So, dream big, then do something about it today!

Reflection Moment of the day:

This day cannot begin without your participation.
<u>Your presence is everything today!</u>

Reflection Moment of the day:

What are the chances that you are the person chosen for a time such as this?!

Reflection Moment of the day:

Sometimes, success means moving in silence.
There is beauty in the silence!

Reflection Moment of the day:

Today,

YOU have an opportunity to **RENEW** in mind, body, and spirit.

It's all up to you!

Reflection Moment of the day:

Keep pushing my friend!
You have come too far to stop now!
Your opportunity awaits!

Reflection Moment of the day:

If there is 1 thing that you can do today, is to be

INTENTIONAL and MOVE!

Let's go!

Reflection Moment of the day:

Don't miss a chance to show up and be great today!

Reflection Moment of the day:

Isn't it about time that you crossed that finish line! Come on! You got it!

Your future depends on it!

Reflection Moment of the day:

HEY,
<u>What are you doing in your Now,</u>
<u>to prepare for YOUR Next?</u>

Reflection Moment of the day:

The Finale!

Reflection Moment of the day

Did you ever think that maybe now is a good time to step out on faith?

Thank you for your support!

Follow me for more:
@Renew_theview

- Coaching services
- Journals
- Coloring books
- And more!

Hey, I'm on Amazon also!

Feel free to leave a review. I appreciate you!
Farrah-

https://Renewtheview.co

As the Founder of **Renew the View, LLC.**, Farrah Brown is delighted to offer mindset and wellness coaching to individuals today. Using her God-gifts, Farrah's mission is to encourage clients to challenge their mindset and shift their focus to reach their goals. Through her coaching services, journals, books, and others products, Farrah is eager to motivate and inspire others to renew their view to become the best version of themselves today! @Renewtheview

Milton Keynes UK
Ingram Content Group UK Ltd.
UKHW041818301123
433549UK00001B/3